SUPER SIMPLE
SCIENCE AT WORK

SUPER SIMPLE
EXPERIMENTS
WITH
FORCES

FUN AND INNOVATIVE SCIENCE PROJECTS

PAIGE V. POLINSKY

CONSULTING EDITOR, DIANE CRAIG, M.A./READING SPECIALIST

Super Sandcastle

An Imprint of Abdo Publishing
abdopublishing.com

abdopublishing.com

Published by Abdo Publishing, a division of ABDO, PO Box 398166, Minneapolis, Minnesota 55439. Copyright © 2017 by Abdo Consulting Group, Inc. International copyrights reserved in all countries. No part of this book may be reproduced in any form without written permission from the publisher. Super SandCastle™ is a trademark and logo of Abdo Publishing.

Printed in the United States of America, North Mankato, Minnesota
062016
092016

THIS BOOK CONTAINS RECYCLED MATERIALS

Editor: Liz Salzmann
Content Developer: Nancy Tuminelly
Cover and Interior Design and Production: Mighty Media, Inc.
Photo Credits: Mighty Media, Inc.; Shutterstock

The following manufacturers/names appearing in this book are trademarks:
Gourmet House®, Pyrex®, Westcott™

Library of Congress Cataloging-in-Publication Data

Names: Polinsky, Paige V., author.
Title: Super simple experiments with forces : fun and innovative science
   projects / Paige V. Polinsky ; consulting editor, Diane Craig,
   M.A./reading specialist.
Description: Minneapolis, Minnesota : Abdo Publishing, [2017] |
   Series: Super simple science at work
Identifiers: LCCN 2016006221 (print) | LCCN 2016014810 (ebook) | ISBN
   9781680781694 (print) | ISBN 9781680776126 (ebook)
Subjects: LCSH: Force and energy--Experiments--Juvenile literature. |
   Science--Experiments--Juvenile literature. | Science projects--Juvenile
   literature.
Classification: LCC QC73.4 .P65 2016 (print) | LCC QC73.4 (ebook) | DDC
   531.113--dc23
LC record available at http://lccn.loc.gov/2016006221

Super SandCastle™ books are created by a team of professional educators, reading specialists, and content developers around five essential components—phonemic awareness, phonics, vocabulary, text comprehension, and fluency—to assist young readers as they develop reading skills and strategies and increase their general knowledge. All books are written, reviewed, and leveled for guided reading and early reading intervention programs for use in shared, guided, and independent reading and writing activities to support a balanced approach to literacy instruction.

To Adult Helpers

The projects in this title are fun and simple. There are just a few things to remember to keep kids safe. Some projects require the use of sharp or hot objects. Also, kids may be using messy materials such as glue or paint. Make sure they protect their clothes and work surfaces. Review the projects before starting, and be ready to assist when necessary.

KEY SYMBOL

Watch for this warning symbol in this book. Here is what it means.

HOT!
You will be working with something hot. Get help!

CONTENTS

FORCES
AT WORK

What happens when you drop something? It falls to the ground, right? Think about some other actions. Stretching a rubber band. Pushing magnets together. Riding your bike. These are all examples of forces at work!

A force is a push or pull that changes something's motion or energy. Forces work in many different ways.

Some forces are at work all the time. Others need certain conditions to work.

TENSION

DRAG

TYPES OF FORCES

There are many types of forces. Gravity is a force that pulls objects toward Earth. It causes things to fall when dropped. Magnetism is another force. Certain metals are magnetic. This means they **attract** other magnets.

Tension and drag are also forces. You feel drag when you ride your bike on a windy day. And you can feel tension in the *snap!* of a stretched rubber band.

NEWTON'S
LAWS

Scientist Sir Isaac Newton discovered laws about forces and motion. His first law is about still objects. It says they will stay still until a force acts on them. For example, a soccer ball is still until it is kicked. The force of the kick makes the ball move.

Newton's second law is about forces and speed. It explains that if the same force pushes two objects, the lighter one will move faster.

This law also says it takes more force to move a heavy object than a light one. That's why it is harder to push a full shopping cart than an empty one.

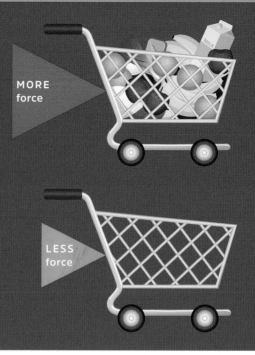

MORE force

LESS force

Newton's third law says that forces act in pairs. This means that every force creates an opposite **reaction**. This can be seen in the way a fish swims. Its fins push water back. The force pushes the fish forward!

WORK LIKE
A SCIENTIST

You've learned about forces and motion. Now you're ready to experiment! Scientists have a special way of working. It is called the Scientific Method. Follow the steps to work like a scientist. It's super simple!

THE SCIENTIFIC METHOD

Have a notebook and pencil handy. Scientists write down everything that happens in their experiments. They also write down their thoughts and ideas.

1. QUESTION

What question are you trying to answer? Write down your question. Then do some **research** to find out more about it.

2. GUESS

Try to guess the answer to your question. Write down your guess.

MICHAEL FARADAY

Michael Faraday started as an assistant to a man who made books. Faraday read the books he made. Some were science books. Later, Faraday became a scientist himself. He is best known for his work with electricity and magnets. Faraday also created the first electric motor that worked.

3. EXPERIMENT

Create an experiment to help answer your question. Write down the steps. Make a list of the supplies you'll need. Then do the experiment. Write down what happens.

4. ANALYSIS

Study the results of your experiment. Did it answer your question? Was your guess correct?

5. CONCLUSION

Think about how the experiment went. Why was your guess wrong or right? Write down the reasons.

MATERIALS

Here are some of the materials that you will need for the experiments in this book.

BROOM	CHENILLE STEMS	CLEAR TAPE	COFFEE FILTERS	COLORED MARKERS	CRAFT FOAM

DISH SOAP	DRINKING GLASS	FOOD COLORING	FUNNEL	HOLE PUNCH	HOT GLUE GUN & GLUE STICKS

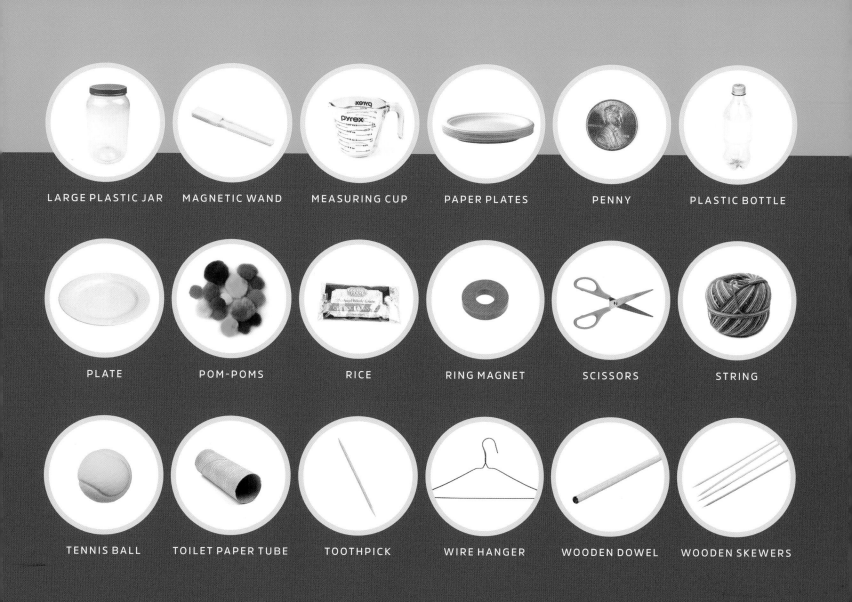

LARGE PLASTIC JAR

MAGNETIC WAND

MEASURING CUP

PAPER PLATES

PENNY

PLASTIC BOTTLE

PLATE

POM-POMS

RICE

RING MAGNET

SCISSORS

STRING

TENNIS BALL

TOILET PAPER TUBE

TOOTHPICK

WIRE HANGER

WOODEN DOWEL

WOODEN SKEWERS

RICE
LIFT

MATERIALS: rice, funnel, plastic bottle, wooden dowel, wooden skewer

Friction is a force. It is created when two surfaces slide across each other. Every surface creates friction. When an object moves across a surface, friction slows it down. The object can even get stuck if the friction is strong enough!

WHY IT WORKS

Tapping the bottle pushes the grains of rice closer together. So does using the dowel. The skewer presses the rice against the sides of the bottle. The grains also rub against each other and the skewer. This creates a lot of friction. It is strong enough to let you lift the whole bottle!

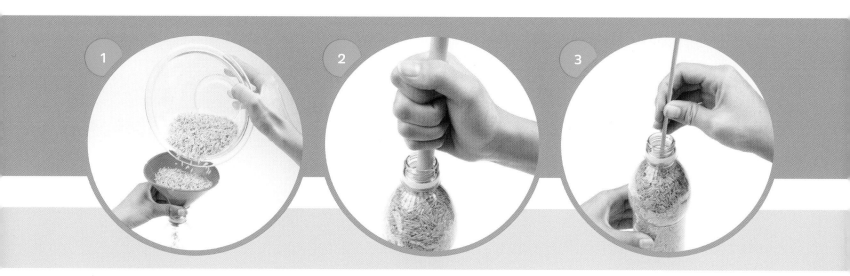

LIFT A LOAD USING FRICTION!

1 Use the funnel to fill the bottle with rice. Put the cap on the bottle. Then firmly tap the bottom of the bottle against a sturdy surface. Repeat many times.

2 Take the cap off the bottle. Use the wooden dowel to push the rice down.

3 Slowly push the skewer into the bottle. Stop when it hits the bottom of the bottle.

4 Hold the skewer and gently lift up. The entire bottle should lift into the air!

PAPER PARACHUTE

MATERIALS: small toy, coffee filter, colored markers (optional), ruler, hole punch, string, scissors

Gravity forces all objects to fall toward Earth. But different objects fall at different speeds. The shape of an object can affect how fast it falls. A narrow object will fall faster than a wide object that weighs the same. This is caused by a force called drag.

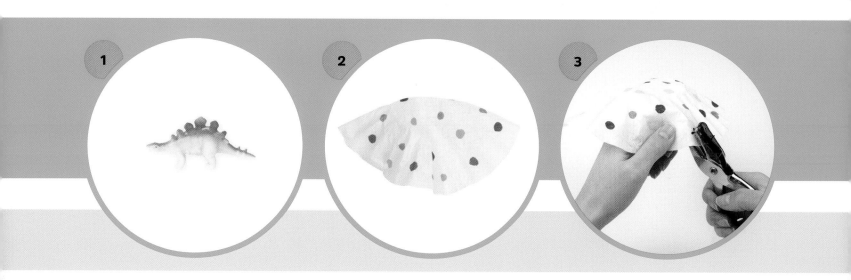

TEST THE FORCE OF GRAVITY!

1 Drop the toy from a high place or throw it into the air. Observe how quickly it falls to the ground.

2 Flatten the coffee filter. Decorate it with markers if you want.

3 Punch four holes about ½ inch (1.3 cm) from the edge of the filter. Be sure to space them evenly.

Continued on the next page.

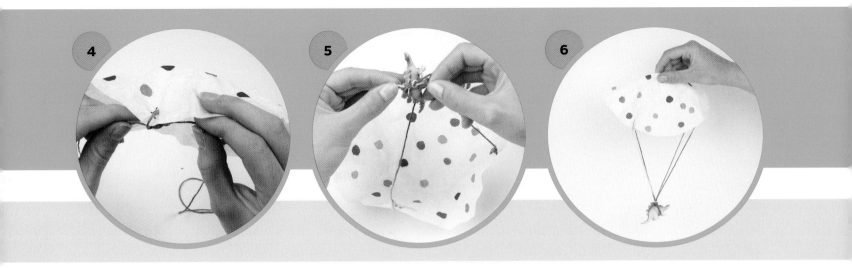

PAPER PARACHUTE (CONTINUED)

4 Cut four pieces of string 16 inches (41 cm) long. Tie one end of each string to a hole in the filter.

5 Tie the other end of each string around the toy.

6 Drop the toy from the same height as before. It should fall to the ground more slowly!

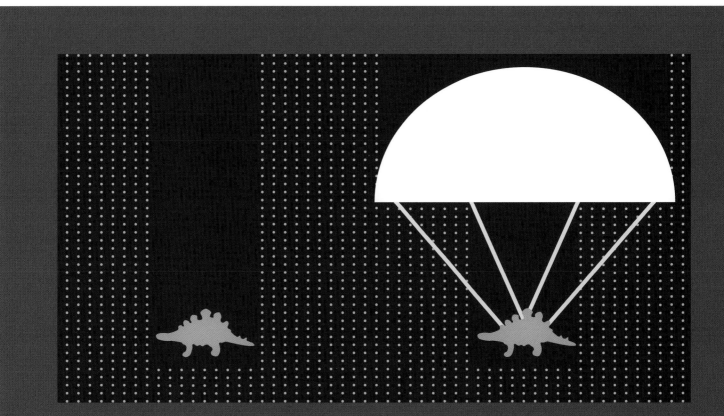

WHY IT WORKS

The toy by itself is narrow. It falls through the air easily. The added coffee filter changes the object's shape. The wide filter has to push more air out of the way. This creates drag. So, even though the object's weight doesn't change, it falls more slowly.

TENNIS BALL
TUMBLE

MATERIALS: drinking glass, paper plate, empty toilet paper tube, tennis ball, broom

Newton's first law says an object will move only if a force acts on it. Test it out with this trick! Use tension and gravity to move a tennis ball!

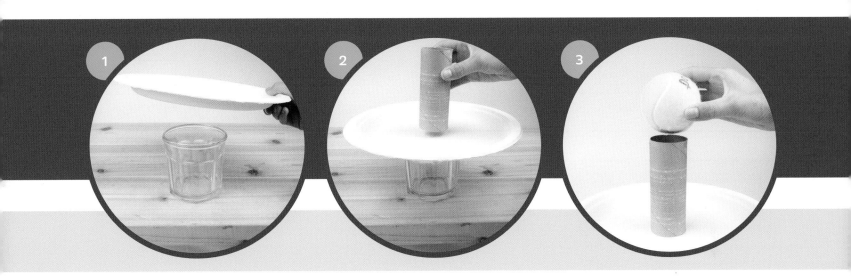

USE FORCES TO CATCH A TENNIS BALL!

1 Set the glass on a table or counter. The glass should be close to the edge. Put the paper plate on top of the glass.

2 Place the toilet paper tube upright on the plate. Make sure it is over the glass.

3 Put the tennis ball on top of the toilet paper tube.

Continued on the next page.

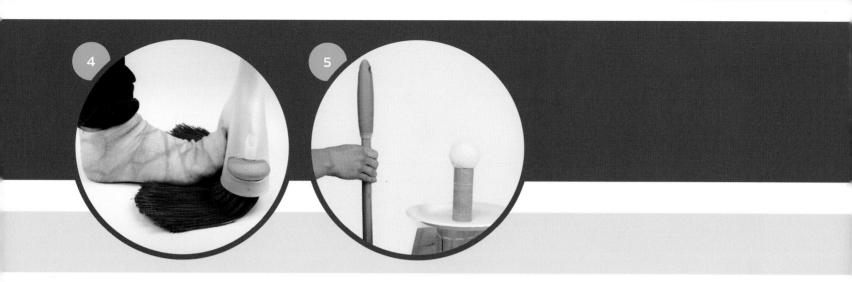

TENNIS BALL TUMBLE (CONTINUED)

④ Stand up the broom near the table. The handle should be at least as tall as the plate. Step on the broom's **bristles**. Press your toes against the broom head.

⑤ Pull the handle back as far as you can. You will feel increased tension in your fingertips and toes.

⑥ Let go. The handle will smack the plate and toilet paper tube away. But the tennis ball should fall into the glass!

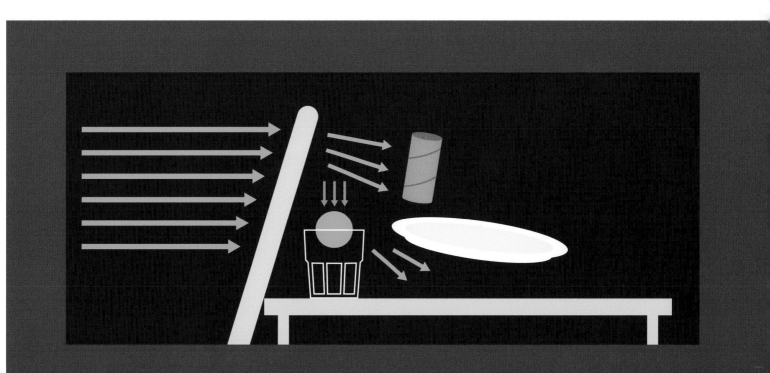

WHY IT WORKS

There is more than one force at work here. Pulling the broom back creates tension. Letting the handle go **releases** this force. It is **transferred** to the paper plate. The paper plate is knocked away. The toilet paper tube moves because it is touching the paper plate. The other force at work is gravity. The broom does not touch the tennis ball. Instead, gravity takes over after the toilet paper tube is gone. The ball drops straight down into the cup!

STICKY
PENNY SWING

The term *centripetal* means "center-seeking." This force makes an object move in a circle. You can feel it on a roller coaster. It presses you into your seat when the ride goes upside-down. And you can use it to perform neat tricks!

WHY IT WORKS

So what keeps the penny from flying off? Spinning the hanger creates a circle. Your finger acts as the center. Centripetal force always pushes toward the center. This means the hook pushes toward your finger. The hook then pushes against the penny. The force keeps the coin in place.

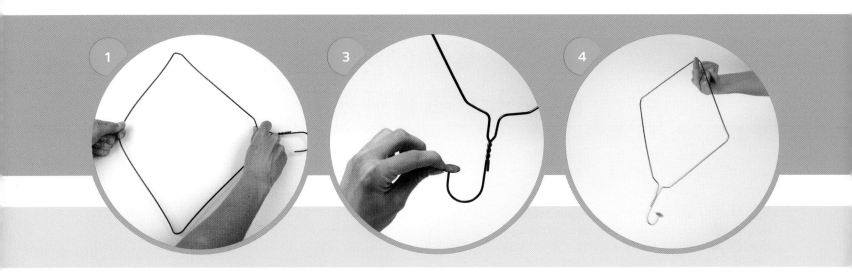

USE FORCES TO BALANCE A PENNY!

① Pull the top and bottom of the hanger apart. Keep pulling until the hanger forms a diamond shape.

② Set the bottom point of the hanger on your finger.

③ Carefully balance the penny on the tip of the hook. Begin swinging the hanger slowly. Move it in a circle.

④ Slowly stop spinning the hanger. The penny should stay on the hook!

FUZZY MAGNET
MATCH-UP

MATERIALS: about 20 pom-poms (4 colors), 4 ring magnets, large plastic jar with lid, hot glue gun & glue sticks, 12 chenille stems (same colors as the pom-poms), scissors, magnetic wand

Magnetic force works all around us. We use it to stick objects to refrigerators. We use it to run microwave ovens. Magnetic forces pull magnets together. Strong forces can pull metal objects without touching them!

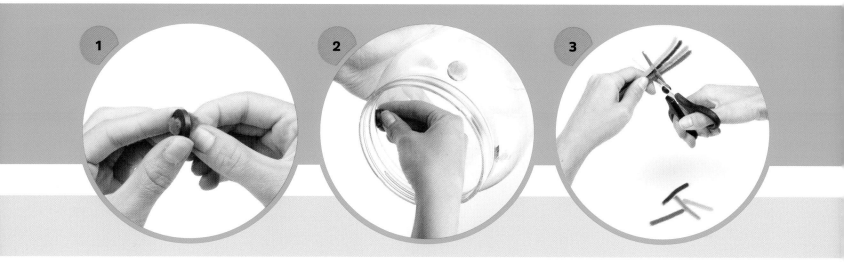

PLAY A GAME WITH MAGNETIC FORCE!

1 Push a small pom-pom through each ring magnet. Use a different color for each one.

2 Hot glue the ring magnets to the inside of the jar. Space them evenly beneath the rim. Let the glue dry.

3 Cut the chenille stems into short pieces.

Continued on the next page.

FUZZY MAGNET MATCH-UP (CONTINUED)

4 Put the rest of the pom-poms in the jar. Add the chenille stem pieces. Put the lid on the jar. Shake the jar to mix the pom-poms and chenille stems.

5 Run the magnetic wand over the outside of the jar. The stem pieces should follow it.

6 Now the game begins! Try to drag each colored stem to its matching magnet. See how many you can match up!

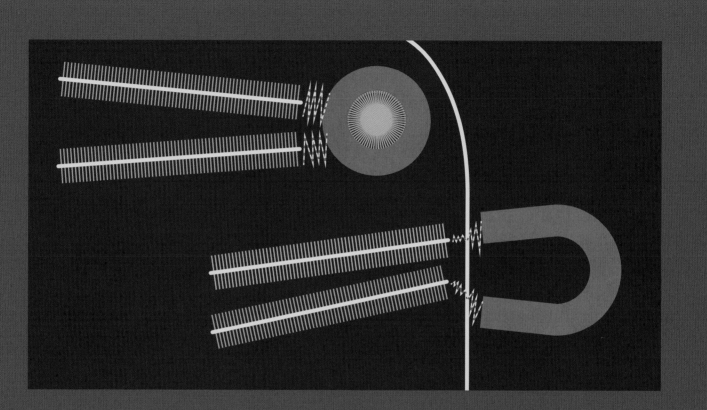

WHY IT WORKS

The chenille stems have metal wires inside them. The wire is magnetic. It is **attracted** to the magnetic wand. The force is strong enough to work through the jar. That is why the wand can drag the chenille stems. The chenille stems are also attracted to the ring magnets. The stems stay put once they touch the ring magnets. The pom-poms aren't magnetic, so they don't move.

SOAPY SAILING

MATERIALS: water, measuring cup, blue food coloring, plate, craft foam, scissors, clear tape, toothpick, dish soap

Water can be broken down into tiny pieces called **molecules**. The molecules stick together on all sides. But those on top have nothing above them. This causes them to hold tighter to the molecules next to and beneath them. The force **attracting** the surface molecules to each other is called surface tension.

MOVE A BOAT WITH SOAP!

1 Fill a measuring cup with water. Add a drop of blue food coloring.

2 Fill the bottom of the plate with the water. Be careful not to let it **overflow**.

3 Cut a rectangle out of craft foam.

4 Cut a small triangle out of craft foam. Tape it to the end of a toothpick.

Continued on the next page.

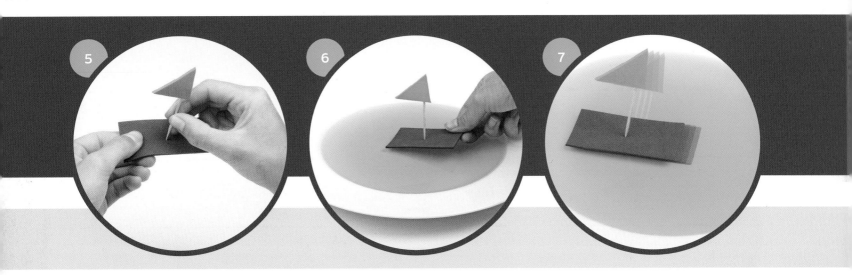

SOAPY SAILING (CONTINUED)

⑤ Gently stick the toothpick into the middle of the foam rectangle. Your boat is now ready!

⑥ Set the boat on the water. Put it in the middle of the plate.

⑦ Put a drop of dish soap right behind the boat. The boat should sail quickly away!

WHY IT WORKS

At first, the water has equal surface tension on all sides of the boat. That keeps the boat in place. But adding the soap changes things. The water **molecules** near the soap separate from each other. This breaks the surface tension of the water behind the boat. The greater tension in front of the boat pulls on the boat. The boat moves forward!

GLOSSARY

attract – to cause someone or something to come near.

bristle – a short, stiff hair or something similar to a hair.

molecule – a group of two or more atoms that make up the smallest piece of a substance.

overflow – to spill over the top.

reaction – an action or movement of one force or object that is caused by the action or movement of another force or object.

release – to set free or let go.

research – the act of finding out more about something.

transfer – to pass from one thing or place to another.